Jesus, Light of the World
An Advent Candle Devotional

Ronda Davenport

ISBN: 1540585034
ISBN-13: 978-1540585035

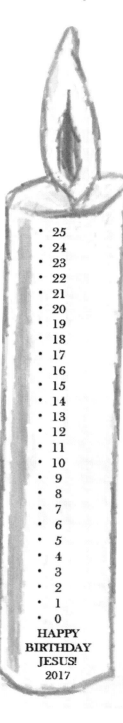

Many years ago, our daughter's kindergarten teacher gave her a beautiful Christmas gift - a booklet of Scriptures and a numbered candle. Each day that December, we gathered as a family and read the scripture for the day by the light of the candle and then took turns praying about the verses. These prayers were simple at first. "Thank you, Jesus, for being the light of the world," little voices would pray. We continued this tradition year after year, and as our children grew, so did their prayers! This became a time of praise and worship to Jesus for His indescribable gift of salvation. Rich conversations about the true meaning of Christmas developed into this devotional book.

At the heart of Christmas is love. God's love for us compelled Him to send His Son. Christ's love for us caused Him to leave His home in Heaven to be born as a little baby. Our love for Jesus, in response to His great love for us, should lead us to give Him our praise and worship, not just at Christmas but all through the year. We are often so distracted that we fail to love God with all of our hearts, souls, minds, and strength as He deserves. This Christmas, give God the gift that He most desires, your heart.

To prepare your advent candle, you will need a taper candle, a sharpie, and a candle holder. Starting at the top of the candle, number from 25 down to 0 in descending order. You may want to put a dot next to each number and write the year and "Happy Birthday Jesus" at the bottom of the candle. Beginning on December 1st, light the candle, and let it burn down until the first dot and number are gone. As it is burning, read the Scripture and devotion for the day. Let one more number and dot burn away daily as you read and pray until Christmas day. As you countdown the days until Christmas, ask God to help you to fall more and more in love with Him. Give Him the gift of a heart full of love and praise. Our family is praying for you that God will greatly bless you as you spend time with Him reading His Word this Christmas season.

"For God so loved the world that He gave His only begotten son that whoever believes in Him should not perish, but have everlasting life."
John 3:16

The True Light

DECEMBER 1
24 DAYS UNTIL CHRISTMAS

In the beginning was the Word, and the Word was with God, and the Word was God. He was with God in the beginning. Through Him all things were made; without Him nothing was made that has been made. In Him was life, and that life was the light of men. The light shines in darkness, but the darkness has not understood it.
John 1:1-5

"The true light that gives light to every man was coming into the world. He was in the world, and though the world was made through Him, the world did not recognize Him. He came to that which was His own, but His own did not recognize Him. He came to that which was His own, but His own did not receive Him. Yet to all who received Him, to those who believed in His name, He gave the right to become children of God- children born not of natural descent, nor of human decision or a husband's will, but born of God. The word became flesh and made His dwelling among us. We have seen His glory, the glory of the One and Only, who came from the Father, full of grace and truth."
John 1:9-14

The miracle of Christmas is this: Jesus Christ, our creator and the creator of our universe, left His home in Heaven to be humbly born into the very world that He created! He came to be the only true light for us, a light that would shine in our dark world and lead us to a relationship with God. Many of the very ones He created did not believe that He was God's Son. Yet, those who did believe were given the right to be called children of God. Things haven't changed much since Jesus' time. Many people still do not recognize Him as the Savior of the world, but, for those who do believe, the gift of salvation is the greatest Christmas gift ever given! Have you received this first Christmas gift that God gave to the world? If you haven't, pray to Jesus and ask Him to be YOUR Savior. Tell Him that you believe that He came into the world, died on the cross, and was raised from the dead, all so that your sins could be forgiven, allowing you to have a relationship with God. That's what Jesus wants for Christmas...your heart! As you celebrate Christmas, spend some time thanking Him for the enormous sacrifice He made for you. He longs for your worship and praise. He knows that when you focus your love and passion on Him, everything else in your life will fall into place.

Prayer and Praise:

_____

_____

_____

_____

_____

_____

_____

_____

_____

_____

_____

_____

_____

Savior of the World

DECEMBER 2
23 DAYS UNTIL CHRISTMAS

So the Lord God said to the serpent, "Because you have done this,
Cursed are you above all the livestock and all the wild animals! You
will crawl on your belly and you will eat dust all the days of your life.
And I will put enmity between you and the woman, and between
your offspring and hers; he will crush your head, and you will strike
his heel."
Genesis 3:14-15

In this passage of scripture, God is speaking about the
consequences of the sin committed by Adam and Eve when they ate
the fruit from the Tree of The Knowledge of Good and Evil. It is
also, however, a biblical prophecy of the birth, death and resurrection
of Jesus Christ. Because Jesus was born as God, wrapped up in the
flesh of man, He is Eve's offspring. Satan, with the sin he brought
into the world, was able to strike the heel of Christ- not a fatal blow.
It did bring Jesus agonizing pain on the cross, but three days later He
rose from the grave! This crushed the head of Satan, leaving him
powerless against those who have been washed by the blood of
Christ. God used prophetic passages to tell people in the past of the
coming of Jesus, the Messiah. Today, we can look back at all of these
prophecies and see that there is only one person in all of history who
has ever fulfilled each and every one…Jesus! As you prepare your

heart for Christmas, remember that, because of the prophecies of the Bible, you can know for certain that baby Jesus, born in the stable in Bethlehem, truly is the One and Only Savior of the world! Thank Him for the gift of His perfect, infallible Word, the Bible!

Prayer and Praise:

_____

_____

_____

_____

_____

_____

_____

_____

_____

_____

_____

_____

_____

_____

_____

_____

_____

_____

_____

_____

_____

_____

_____

_____

_____

_____

_____

_____

Perfect Sacrifice

DECEMBER 3
22 DAYS UNTIL CHRISTMAS

Sometime later God tested Abraham. He said to him, 'Abraham!' 'Here I am,' he replied. Then God said, 'take your son, your only son, Isaac, whom you love, and go to the region of Moriah. Sacrifice him there as a burnt offering on one of the mountains I will tell you about. Early the next morning Abraham got up and saddled his donkey. He took with him two of his servants and his son Isaac. When he had cut enough wood for the burnt offering, he set out for the place God had told him about. On the third day, Abraham looked up and saw the place in the distance. He said to his servants, 'Stay here with the donkey while I and the boy go over there. We will worship and then we will come back to you. Abraham took the wood for the burnt offering and placed it on his son Isaac, and he himself carried the fire and the knife. As the two of them went on together, Isaac spoke up and said to his father Abraham, 'Father?' 'Yes, my son?' Abraham replied. 'The fire and wood are here,' Isaac said, 'but where is the lamb for the burnt offering?' Abraham answered, 'God himself will provide the lamb for the burnt offering, my son. And the two of them went on together.
Genesis 22:1-8

This account of the testing of Abraham's willingness to obey God, whatever the cost, is an incredible testimony of Abraham's faith in the Lord. It is also a prophecy of another son who would have to be given up as the perfect sacrifice for sin. When God told Abraham to take his only son whom he loved and sacrifice him as a temporary atonement for sin, God already knew that He would one day willingly give His own son, whom He loved, as the permanent sacrifice for our sins. When Isaac asked his father where the lamb for the burnt offering was, Abraham told his son that God himself would provide the lamb. As with many prophecies, this statement was fulfilled in the near future through the ram caught in a bramble. Later, this prophecy is fulfilled permanently through the Lamb that is our perfect, sinless, blameless, Savior, Jesus! Christmas is all about God's willingness to send His Son to us, and Jesus' willingness to come. If the first Christmas had never happened, we would not have the eternal hope that salvation brings. Christmas can be a busy time filled with wonderful celebrations. Never rob yourself by allowing the busyness to overshadow the true meaning, the true reason to celebrate. Jesus is the heart and life of Christmas. Don't forget to invite Him to be a part of His own birthday party. Ask Him to be the biggest part of your holiday, and you will enjoy the true blessings that this Holy day holds.

Prayer and Praise:

_____

_____

_____

_____

_____

_____

_____

_____

_____

_____

_____

Passover Lamb

DECEMBER 4
21 DAYS UNTIL CHRISTMAS

Then Moses summoned all the elders of Israel and said to them, "Go at once and select the animals for your families and slaughter the Passover Lamb. Take a bunch of hyssop, dip it into the blood in the basin and put some of the blood on the top and on both sides of the doorframe. Not one of you shall go out the door of his house until morning. When the Lord goes through the land to strike down the Egyptians, he will see the blood on the top and sides of the doorframe and will pass over that doorway, and he will not permit the destroyer to enter your houses and strike you down.
Exodus 12:21-23

Passover is the Jewish celebration of the final plague that God sent when the Israelites were slaves in Egypt. God's judgment on Egypt was demonstrated by the death of the firstborn son of every household. The only escape was for a household to have marked the doorway with the blood of the Passover Lamb. Can you imagine the sadness of the Egyptian parents when they woke up to find their oldest son dead? This was the last of ten plagues that God sent in order to convince Pharaoh to let the Israelites go. The plagues had become increasingly worse, giving the Egyptians chance after chance to believe in the One True God and obey. They were warned before each and every plague of the consequence disobedience would bring, and still they did not believe. Today, Jesus is our Passover Lamb sacrificed once for all of our sins. His blood, shed on the cross for us, gives us the opportunity to get ready for death and eternity. Like the Egyptians, we are given many chances to believe and obey God. Have you ever had the feeling inside that you knew you needed to ask Christ to forgive you for the wrong things you've done and be your Savior? What did you do about that feeling? Each time you have that feeling, Jesus is giving you another chance to accept Him. He has told us in His Word that the consequence of sin is death, yet because of His great love for us, God provided for us His son as our Passover Lamb. Because of their stubbornness and self-reliance, there was not a happy ending for the Egyptians. Aren't you thankful that there can be a happy ending for us? Thank Jesus for being your Passover Lamb today!

Prayer and Praise:

_____

_____

_____

_____

_____

_____

_____

_____

_____

_____

_____

_____

_____

_____

_____

_____

_____

_____

Gentle Shepherd

DECEMBER 5
20 DAYS UNTIL CHRISTMAS

A voice of one calling: "In the desert prepare the way for the LORD; make straight in the wilderness a highway for our God. Every valley shall be raised up, every mountain and hill made low; the rough ground shall become level, the rugged places a plain. And the glory of the LORD will be revealed, and all mankind together will see it. For the mouth of the LORD has spoken." A voice says, "Cry out." And I said, "What shall I cry?" "All men are like grass, and all their glory is like the flowers of the field. The grass withers and the flowers fall, because the breath of the LORD blows on them. Surely the people are grass. The grass withers and the flowers fall, but the word of our God stands forever." You who bring good tidings to Zion, go up on a high mountain. You who bring good tidings to Jerusalem, lift up your voice with a shout, lift it up, do not be afraid; say to the towns of Judah, "Here is your God!" See, the Sovereign LORD comes with power and his arm rules for him. See, his reward is with him, and his recompense accompanies him. He tends his flock like a shepherd: He gathers the lambs in his arms and carries them close to his heart; he gently leads those that have young.
Isaiah 40:3-11

Isaiah gives us a prophetic look at a person who will come before Christ and prepare the way for Him, John the Baptist. Like John, Isaiah is the prophet of his time whom God uses to call people to prepare the way for the Lord. As your family gets ready for holiday guests to come to your home, there are many preparations that must be made. If you are like me, you will probably spend some time cleaning up for your company! We like for things to be neat and tidy when our friends and family arrive. Isaiah encourages us to prepare ourselves spiritually in response to the two historical events that are prophesied in this passage. The first event is the first coming of Christ, which happened when Jesus was born. The second event, mentioned in the last part of the passage, will happen in the future when Christ returns for His church. Our hearts need to be clean and free from sin so that we will be ready for God's Son when He comes again. What does it mean to be ready? First and foremost, it means believing that we have the need for our sins to be forgiven and asking Jesus to forgive them. I can't very well clean my house if I don't realize that it is dirty. In the same way, Christ does not cleanse us from our sins until we recognize our need for forgiveness and ask Him to be our Savior. Once we ask Jesus to be the Lord of our lives, WE become the voices of ones calling in our world to prepare the way for the LORD. Our world needs to know that, although our lives are as temporary as the grass, God is everlasting. He seeks to gently shepherd us and carry us close to His heart while we are here on Earth and for all of eternity in Heaven. Who is God asking you to share the message of Jesus with during this Christmas season? "Lift up your voice with a shout, lift it up, do not be afraid, say to [your town,] here is your God!"

Prayer and Praise:

_____

_____

_____

_____

_____

_____

Son of God

DECEMBER 6
19 DAYS UNTIL CHRISTMAS

"I baptize with water," John replied, "but among you stands one you do not know. He is the one who comes after me, the thongs of whose sandals I am not worthy to untie." This all happened at Bethany on the other side of the Jordan, where John was baptizing. The next day John saw Jesus coming toward him and said, "look, the Lamb of God, who takes away the sin of the world! This is the one I meant when I said, 'A man who comes after me has surpassed me because he was before me.' I myself did not know him, but the reason I came baptizing with water was that he might be revealed to Israel." Then John gave this testimony: "I saw the Spirit come down from Heaven as a dove and remain on him. I would not have known him, except that the one who sent me to baptize with water told me, 'The man on whom you see the Spirit come down and remain is he who will baptize with the Holy Spirit.' I have seen and I testify that this is the Son of God.
John 1:26-34

When John started preaching that people needed to repent because the Messiah was coming, the priests and Levites decided to find out who John was. Some thought that he himself was the Messiah. Others thought that he was Elijah (Malachi 4:5) or the prophet predicted by Moses (Deuteronomy 18:15). John quickly dispelled these thoughts. He claimed only to be the "voice of one calling in the desert, 'make straight the way for the Lord.'" He did not want anyone to attribute greatness to him, but to Christ alone. John mentioned that he baptized with water in contrast to Jesus who would baptize with the Holy Spirit. He further illustrated his humility by telling them that he was not even worthy to untie Jesus' sandals, an act usually reserved for the lowliest of servants. When John saw Jesus coming, he told the crowd that God the Father had revealed to him that Jesus was God the Son. Being born after John, Jesus was before John because He had existed for all of eternity. John never grew weary of pointing people to Jesus. He never faltered in giving all of the glory to God. He had a personal relationship with the Messiah, the one sent to take away the sin of the world. How could he not tell others who Christ was? If we have asked Christ to be our Savior, we have that same personal relationship with the Messiah. He really is the ONE sent to take away the sin of the people who are living in the world with us right now! How can we not tell them who He is? Tell someone today, "I have seen, and I testify that [Jesus] is the Son of God!"

Prayer and Praise:

_____

_____

_____

_____

_____

_____

_____

_____

_____

_____

_____

_____

_____

Deliverer

DECEMBER 7
18 DAYS UNTIL CHRISTMAS

Just as Moses lifted up the snake in the desert, so the Son of Man
must be lifted up, that everyone who believes in Him may have
eternal life. "For God so loved the world that He gave His One and
Only Son, that whoever believes in Him shall not perish but have
eternal life. For God did not send His Son into the world to
condemn the world, but to save the world through Him.
John 3:14-17

Numbers 21:4-9 tells the story of the Israelites as they wandered
through the desert looking for the promised land. Even though God
had brought them out of slavery and bondage in Egypt, parted the
Red Sea so they could cross on dry land, and provided for all of their
needs as they traveled, "they spoke against God." They forgot all that
God had done for them and complained about their current
situation. The Bible says that the LORD sent venomous snakes
among them; they bit the people and many Israelites died. Realizing
their sin, they asked Moses to pray that the LORD would take the
snakes away. In His great mercy, God instructed Moses to make a
snake and put it up on a pole so that when anyone was bitten they
could look at the snake and live. This event is a picture of Christ. Just
as the Israelites would have died from their snakebites without God's
merciful deliverance, the result of our sinfulness, apart from Christ, is

death. Jesus, the Son of Man, lived a perfect, sinless life. He did not deserve to be "lifted up" on the cross of Calvary to die an excruciating death. He took my place. He took your place. Jesus bore the judgment for our sins so that we could choose to have a relationship with God through Him. God's gift to us is ETERNAL LIFE, yet how often do we forget about this incredible gift and become discontent with our circumstances? It is so easy for us to see now that the Israelites should have trusted that God knew what He was doing during those difficult desert days. He had proven His love and faithfulness to them time and time again. It is harder for us to realize that we too need to trust God during our desert days, but think how much more He has proven His love and faithfulness to us through the person of His One and Only Son! May this Christmas be a time, like never before, of remembrance and thankfulness that God did not send His Son into the world to condemn the world, but to save the world through Him.

Prayer and Praise:

_____

_____

_____

_____

_____

_____

_____

_____

_____

_____

_____

_____

_____

_____

_____

_____

Immanuel

DECEMBER 8
17 DAYS UNTIL CHRISTMAS

Therefore the Lord himself will give you a sign: The virgin will be with child and will give birth to a son, and will call him Immanuel.
Isaiah 7:14

This prophecy came 740 years before the time that the angel Gabriel visited Mary and told her that she would be with child and give birth to a Son, who she was to name Jesus. Like many prophecies, this one had an application in Isaiah's day, but was only completely fulfilled when Christ was born centuries later. When God gave Isaiah these words, He was dealing with the stubborn King Ahaz. God was trying to speak through Isaiah to give Ahaz, king of Judah, Godly instructions concerning a political alliance he was considering. God did not want Ahaz to make this alliance, asking him to trust God for protection. God told Ahaz to ask for a sign that He would protect Judah, but Ahaz would not ask. God decided to give Ahaz a sign even though he refused to ask for one. The sign was that a young woman who was betrothed to Isaiah, and still a virgin, would soon marry Isaiah and give birth to his son. The name that was given to their son was to be Immanuel, which means God is with us. This name was meant to show Ahaz that he could count on God to rescue him from his enemies without entering into an unwise coalition with other countries. In God's sovereign wisdom, He knew that the words

He gave Isaiah would have a greater and deeper meaning 740 years later when the virgin Mary would give birth to Immanuel, who is God with all of mankind, not just Judah. God's plan for redemption was set into motion when sin entered the world through Adam and Eve. Christ's virgin birth, death, burial, and resurrection laid out the plan for salvation from sin. Many prophesies are being fulfilled in our present day that point to the second coming of Christ. Throughout the history of our world, God has been faithful to fulfill the prophesies in His Word. Christ was born of a virgin just as the Scriptures foretold. He will also come again according to the scriptures. What if He comes today? Are you ready? Have you surrendered your life FULLY to Him? If not, what better gift could you give Him at Christmas than all of yourself!

Prayer and Praise:

_____

_____

_____

_____

_____

_____

_____

_____

_____

_____

_____

_____

_____

_____

_____

_____

_____

_____

Prince of Peace

DECEMBER 9
16 DAYS UNTIL CHRISTMAS

For to us a child is born, to us a Son is given, and the government
will be on his shoulders. And he will be called Wonderful Counselor,
Mighty God, Everlasting Father, Prince of Peace.
Isaiah 9:6

Isaiah describes Jesus' humanity in referring to him as a child and
His deity in calling Him a Son. Therein lies the beauty and majesty of
Christ. He is as much man as He is God, and as much God as He is
man. He did not come to earth to rule, but to serve. He did not come
to exert His authority as God, but to live a perfect, sinless life as a
man. Although Christ willingly relinquished His right to reign and
rule during His life on earth, Isaiah also speaks of a day coming when
the government will be on His shoulders. At that time, when Jesus
returns to earth again, the government as we know it will no longer
exist. Jesus will govern in truth and righteousness as the King of
kings and the Lord of lords! Won't that be different! He will be a
Wonderful Counselor, ruling in wisdom, fairness, and justice. As
Mighty God, His rule will be supreme. No longer will government try
to overthrow government with Christ at the helm. Our Everlasting
Father will tenderly protect and provide for His children for all of
eternity. Jesus, Prince of Peace will bring peace to each and every
heart and to our society as a whole. We have so much to excitedly

anticipate! Just as a child can barely wait for Christmas morning to receive a special gift, we too should be filled with joy thinking about the promises we have in Christ. Why, then, are we often less than enthusiastic about the return of Christ, wanting to experience life or accomplish various goals first? It can only be because we are holding on so tightly to what is good that we are not opening our hands for God to give us what is supremely better. Christmas is about giving. Open your hands wide to give Christ all of your hopes and dreams so that He can place in your empty hands all that He has in store for those who love Him.

Prayer and Praise:

_____

_____

_____

_____

_____

_____

_____

_____

_____

_____

_____

_____

_____

_____

_____

_____

_____

_____

_____

_____

Son of the Most High

DECEMBER 10
15 DAYS UNTIL CHRISTMAS

But the angel said to her, "Do not be afraid, Mary, you have found
favor with God. You will be with child and give birth to a son, and
you are to give him the name Jesus. He will be great and will be called
the Son of the Most High. The Lord God will give him the throne of
his father David, and he will reign over the house of Jacob forever;
his kingdom will never end.
Luke 1:30-33

Wow! What a lot for Mary to take in. God was choosing her to be
the mother of the long-awaited Messiah- the Son of the Most High.
She had found favor with God, so He was allowing her to participate
in His plan of salvation for the world. She gave Jesus His humanity.
Knowing all that we know about what Mary would have to see her
son go through to become the Savior of the world, it is clear that her
favored position did not protect her from sorrow and heartache.
Being involved with the work of God's kingdom in this world is not
always easy. God does not promise that we will not go through
troubles and trials, but He does promise to walk with us through each
one. He promises to never leave us or forsake us. As recipients of the
gift of salvation, forgiveness, and eternal life, we, like Mary, have also
found favor with God. He does not need us to accomplish His work
here on Earth. He is God, after all, completely capable of fulfilling

His purposes in whatever way He chooses. His choice, though, is to allow us to participate in His plan of salvation for the world. We are the ones who are blessed when we obey God's calling on our lives, no matter how difficult that calling may seem. Have you come to the place in your life that you want what God wants more than you want what you want? If not, are you willing to put God's plan above your own? Pray about it today. Ask God to replace your desires with His own. He will do it, and your life will be filled with purpose, meaning and unparalleled passion! Do not be afraid…you have found favor with God!

Prayer and Praise:

_____

_____

_____

_____

_____

_____

_____

_____

_____

_____

_____

_____

_____

_____

_____

_____

_____

_____

_____

Mighty One

DECEMBER 11
14 DAYS UNTIL CHRISTMAS

And Mary said, "My soul glorifies the Lord and my spirit rejoices in God my Savior, for he has been mindful of the humble state of his servant. From now on all generations will call me blessed, for the Mighty One has done great things for me- Holy is His name. His mercy extends to those who fear him, from generation to generation."
Luke 1:46-50

Mary could have responded to the news that she was with child in many understandable ways. She could have been filled with doubt and confusion as to how this could be possible. Instead, she was filled with faith and trust. She could have been fearful of the consequences of being pregnant when she was not yet married. Instead, she was joyful. She could have focused on herself and what all of this meant to her. Instead, she focused on the Lord and what it all meant to Him. Most importantly, Mary praised God for who He is and the part He was allowing her to play in her generation. She didn't get to choose her part. That was up to God. Her choice was in how she would respond. God has a plan for each of us to fulfill in our own time in history. Like Mary, we don't get to come up with the plan, but we do get to decide how we will respond. How will you respond when God reveals part of His plan for your life? Will you respond in obedience with thanksgiving and praise to God even if the plan doesn't make sense from a human perspective? Will you be filled with faith, trust, joy, and devotion to God? The Mighty One has done great things for you- Holy is His name! His mercy extends to you! Praise Him today for who He is and what He is up to in your life.

Prayer and Praise:

_____

_____

_____

_____

_____

_____

_____

_____

_____

_____

_____

_____

_____

_____

_____

_____

_____

_____

_____

_____

_____

_____

_____

_____

_____

Son of David

DECEMBER 12
13 DAYS UNTIL CHRISTMAS

This is how the birth of Jesus Christ came about: His mother Mary
was pledged to be married to Joseph, but before they came together,
she was found to be with child through the Holy Spirit. Because
Joseph her husband was a righteous man and did not want to expose
her public disgrace, he had in mind to divorce her quietly. But after
he had considered this, an angel of the Lord appeared to him in a
dream and said, "Joseph son of David, do not be afraid to take Mary
home as your wife, because what is conceived in her is from the Holy
Spirit. She will give birth to a son, and you are to give him the name
Jesus, because he will save his people from their sins.
Matthew 1:18-21

Mary was pledged to be married to Joseph. They were engaged.
They were not yet living together as husband and wife, but were
considered to be legally bound to one another during this betrothal
period. For this reason, Joseph had a difficult choice to make. He
could have divorced Mary publicly, in which case she would likely
have been stoned, during that time in history, for her assumed
unfaithfulness to Joseph. The Bible tells us that Joseph was a
righteous man, meaning that he was zealous in keeping the law. He
must have also been a compassionate man because he did not want
to submit Mary to public disgrace. His solution was to quietly divorce

her, but then God intervened. An angel of the Lord came to Joseph in a dream confirming that the child Mary was carrying truly was God's son. In obedience to God's voice, Joseph got up the next morning and took Mary home as his wife (verse 24). We are all faced with important decisions and choices. God cares and has an opinion about each one of them! There is always a best answer, but rarely are we able to come to that answer on our own. God sees all from the beginning to the end of time and then on into eternity. His wisdom and knowledge, combined with His desire to give us His very best, make Him the only source we can truly count on when we are faced with a problem and need a Godly solution. Seek God in every decision, no matter how big or small, and then, like Joseph, obey His voice immediately. You may never know until you get to Heaven what a difference your obedience to God will make!

Prayer and Praise:

_____

_____

_____

_____

_____

_____

_____

_____

_____

_____

_____

_____

_____

_____

_____

The Babe born in Bethlehem

DECEMBER 13
12 DAYS UNTIL CHRISTMAS

In those days Caesar Augustus issued a decree that a census should be taken of the entire Roman world. (This was the first census that took place while Quirinius was governor of Syria.) And everyone went to his own town to register. So Joseph also went up from the town of Nazareth in Galilee to Judea, to Bethlehem the town of David, because he belonged to the house and line of David. He went there to register with Mary, who was pledged to be married to him and was expecting a child. While they were there, the time came for the baby to be born, and she gave birth to her firstborn, a son. She wrapped him in cloths and placed him in a manger, because there was no room for them in the inn.
Luke 2:1-7

Isn't God amazing? In Micah 5:2, God used His prophet to reveal the location of the Savior's birth as Bethlehem. Why Bethlehem? Because He knew long, long, before Jesus was ever conceived that Caesar Augustus would issue a decree that a census should be taken requiring Joseph, and a very pregnant Mary, to go to Bethlehem to be counted as part of the house and line of David. God used this pagan emperor to fulfill His prophecy, placing Mary and Joseph in just the right place at just the right time for the birth of Christ. Nothing happens by chance with God! He sees all, knows all, and uses all knowledge as he intricately weaves together the fabric of history. Why wasn't there any room in the inn? Was it beyond God's control to provide a nice place for His son to be born? Absolutely not! He chose a manger as the place Jesus would first sleep. Just as this humble location gave the shepherds access to baby Jesus, it represented the access that all of mankind- rich, poor, weak, and strong- would have to God through Christ. Mary may not have understood, at the time, what God was doing in bringing such a special baby into the world in such a lowly manner. You may not always understand what He is doing in your life either. You are one of the many precious, beautiful threads He is using in His eternal tapestry. Trust Him, and do not lose heart. His design will one day be clear, and you will marvel at His amazing ability to work all of the events in your life into His master plan for the Kingdom of God.

Prayer and Praise:

_____

_____

_____

_____

_____

_____

_____

_____

_____

_____

_____

_____

_____

_____

_____

_____

Christ the Lord

DECEMBER 14
11 DAYS UNTIL CHRISTMAS

And there were shepherds living out in the fields nearby, keeping watch over their flocks at night. An angel of the Lord appeared to them, and the glory of the Lord shone around them, and they were terrified. But the angel said to them, "Do not be afraid. I bring you good news of great joy that will be for all the people. Today in the town of David a Savior has been born to you; He is Christ the Lord. This will be a sign to you: You will find a baby wrapped in cloths and lying in a manger." Suddenly a multitude of the heavenly host appeared with the angel, praising God and saying, "Glory to God in the highest, and on earth peace and good will toward men."
Luke 2:8-14

The very first people to find out about the birth of Jesus were not the religious or political leaders. They were not rich, powerful, or even important in the world's eyes. The shepherds were given the incredible honor of hearing the good news of Christ the Lord before anyone else. Only God knows for certain why He chose the shepherds. Maybe they were just in the right place at the right time. More likely, though, God looked at the hearts of the people and His eyes rested on the humble, faithful shepherds because He knew they were capable of true worship of the baby in the manger. He also knew that they would happily share the good news told to them by the angels with everyone they met. The angels told the shepherds to look for this sign: a baby wrapped in cloths and lying in a manger. Signs were used to validate the truth of the spoken word. It would have been odd to find any baby in a manger, the feeding trough of an animal. No one would ever expect to find the Savior of the world there! The sign would prove the angels right. I drove by a church today with this message on their marquis: Is God looking for a sign from us? This really made me think! If a sign validates the truth of what we say, then what kind of sign could God be looking for? As Christians we have much to say. We say that we love God, but where is the sign? We say that Christ is the Lord of our lives. Is there a sign to validate that? We say that we want the world to know our Savior. Wouldn't a sign be that we are telling them about Him? Ask yourself if God is looking for a sign from you. Is there a sign that validates the truth of your relationship with Jesus? Let us be sure to give God the signs that He is looking for at Christmas time and all year long!

Prayer and Praise:

_____

_____

_____

_____

_____

_____

_____

_____

_____

_____

_____

_____

_____

_____

Good News!

DECEMBER 15
10 DAYS UNTIL CHRISTMAS

When the angels had left them and gone into heaven, the shepherds
said to one another, "Let's go to Bethlehem and see this thing that
has happened, which the Lord has told us about." So they hurried off
and found Mary and Joseph, and the baby, who was lying the manger.
When they had seen him, they spread the word concerning what had
been told them about this child, and all who heard it were amazed at
what the shepherds said to them. But Mary treasured up all these
things and pondered them in her heart. The shepherds returned,
glorifying and praising God for all the things they had heard and
seen, which were just as they had been told.
Luke 2:15-20

I love to imagine the shepherds right after the angels had left them
and gone into heaven. They couldn't wait to get to Bethlehem! They
didn't get a good night's sleep and head to Bethlehem in the
morning. They dropped everything and hurried off. I picture them
running, skipping and dancing their way to find King Jesus in His
manger. Their encounter with God, and the Christ-child, Jesus, left
such an impression on their hearts that they had to tell everyone the
good news! They created quite a commotion in Bethlehem as they
related their experience with such enthusiasm and excitement that the
response from all who heard it was amazement. Even after they
returned to their fields to tend their sheep, they continued to glorify
and praise God for all the things they had heard and seen which were

just as they had been told. I believe that the shepherds were forever changed by the touch of God on their lives, just as anyone who has felt the touch of God should be. You probably see where I am headed with this, don't you? As Christians, we have not only encountered King Jesus, we have His very Spirit living within us! How are we sitting still? How are we not dropping everything to spend time with Him? Why are we not so excited that we are compelled to tell everyone, and so enthusiastic that they are simply amazed by what we have to share? Isn't it time that we create a commotion over our Lord and Savior? You are the only witness who can tell others what Jesus means to you. Spread the good news of Christmas, and wake up this dark and sleeping world to the real reason we have to rejoice!

Prayer and Praise:

_____

_____

_____

_____

_____

_____

_____

_____

_____

_____

_____

_____

_____

_____

_____

_____

Consecrated to the Lord

DECEMBER 16
9 DAYS UNTIL CHRISTMAS

On the eighth day, when it was time to circumcise him, he was named Jesus, the name the angel had given him before he had been conceived. When the time of their purification according to the Law of Moses had been completed, Joseph and Mary took Him to Jerusalem to present Him to the Lord (as it is written in the Law of the Lord, "Every firstborn male is to be consecrated to the Lord"), and to offer a sacrifice in keeping with what is said in the Law of the Lord: "a pair of doves or two young pigeons."
Luke 2:21-24

The Mosaic law gave specific instructions that Mary and Joseph adhered to in the days following the birth of Jesus. The circumcision, which took place when Jesus was eight days old, was a remembrance of the covenant God made with Abraham. It was on the eighth day that they gave Him the name Jesus. The time of purification for Mary was forty days after Jesus' birth. She was actually supposed to bring a lamb and a pigeon or a dove to sacrifice; however, the poor were permitted to bring a pair of doves or two young pigeons. It reveals insight into the financial situation of Jesus' family that Mary and Joseph were too poor to bring the customary sacrifice. The law also required that the first-born son be dedicated to the Lord in the temple. Mary and Joseph followed these laws out of love, honor, and respect for God who had given the laws. Today, because of the shed blood of Jesus for our sins, we no longer live under the law, but under grace. There is no need to make animal sacrifices because Christ died as a permanent sacrifice for our sins. It is still important, though, to study God's Word and follow the teachings found therein. Grace does not allow us to ignore the laws of God; through grace, He extends mercy to us when we sin and fail to live up to the law. The ultimate goal is still to love, honor, and respect God through obedience to His Word. The Bible is the lamp that shows us our sin, but, Jesus is the lamb who died once for all to take away our sin. One way that you love God is by loving His Word. Do you love His Word, the Bible? Does it thrill you to read it and hear from God through its pages? If not, ask Him to give you a greater love for the Scriptures. God's will for you is to love Him and His Word supremely. You can be confident that if you ask for His help in doing His will, He will answer you in ways that you could never imagine!

Prayer and Praise:

_____

_____

_____

_____

_____

_____

_____

_____

_____

_____

_____

_____

_____

_____

_____

_____

_____

_____

Consolation of Israel

DECEMBER 17
8 DAYS UNTIL CHRISTMAS

Now there was a man in Jerusalem called Simeon, who was righteous and devout. He was waiting for the consolation of Israel, and the Holy Spirit was upon him. It had been revealed to him by the Holy Spirit that he would not die before he had seen the Lord's Christ. Moved by the Spirit, he went into the temple courts. When the parents brought in the child Jesus to do for Him what the custom of the Law required, Simeon took Him in his arms and praised God saying: "Sovereign Lord, as you have promised, you now dismiss your servant in peace. For my eyes have seen your salvation, which you have prepared in the sight of all people, a light for revelation to the Gentiles and for glory to your people Israel." The child's father and mother marveled at what was said about Him. Then Simeon blessed them and said to Mary, His mother: "This child is destined to cause the falling and rising of many in Israel, and to be a sign that will be spoken against, so that the thoughts of many hearts will be revealed. And a sword will pierce your own soul too."
Luke 2:25-34

Simeon was chosen by God not only to meet the Christ-child, but to fully comprehend His true identity as the savior and the consolation of Israel. The Bible tells us that the Holy Spirit was upon Simeon. The Spirit gave him the special insight to go to the temple at the time that Mary and Joseph would be there with Jesus, and the discernment to recognize the baby as God's Son, the Savior of the world. As he reached for Jesus and took Him in his arms, I imagine that the tears must have started flowing. Staring into the precious, innocent face of the ONE who had created him must have been absolutely breath-taking! He began to praise God...what an appropriate response, having just gazed into the eyes of Christ! This was the moment Simeon had been waiting for his entire life. He was now able to die in peace knowing that Jesus had finally come for the Jews and for the Gentiles (that's us!) as well. He then blessed Mary and Joseph and turned to Mary with some prophetic words about Jesus' life. He predicted that Jesus would cause the falling and rising of many in Israel. Those who refused to believe in Him would fall to their own sinfulness, while those who embraced the truth of who He was would rise above the sin that held them captive. Simeon also foretold that Jesus would be spoken against, reflecting the hatred that many would have for Him. Jesus would reveal the thoughts of many hearts, testing whether or not they were able to hear the voice of God and see His very nature in the person of Christ. Finally, he told Mary that a sword would pierce her own soul too, indicating that she would suffer greatly as she watched her son suffer. This meeting must have been bittersweet for Mary. How thrilled she must have been for Simeon to confirm the very things that the angel, Gabriel, had spoken to her before Jesus was born. How tormented she must have felt to get a glimpse of the suffering Jesus would have to endure to fulfill God's plan for the salvation of the world. At Christmas, we remember Jesus, the babe in the manger. Praise Him today that He is also Jesus, the Savior who bore the sins of the world on the cross!

Prayer and Praise:

_____

_____

_____

_____

_____

_____

_____

Redemption of Jerusalem

DECEMBER 18
7 DAYS UNTIL CHRISTMAS

There was also a prophetess, Anna, the daughter of Phanuel, of the
tribe of Asher . She was very old; she had lived with her husband
seven years after her marriage, and then was a widow until she was
eighty-four. She never left the temple but worshipped night and day,
fasting and praying. Coming up to them at that very moment, she
gave thanks to God and spoke about the child to all who were
looking forward to the redemption of Jerusalem.
Luke 2:36-38

As Simeon was speaking with Mary, Anna joined the people who
were gathered around Jesus and gave thanks to God. She spoke
about the baby Jesus, the redemption of Jerusalem, to all who would
listen. Like the shepherds, who first heard the good news of Christ's
arrival here on earth, Simeon and Anna were not the religious leaders
of the temple. The Bible does not mention the involvement of the
religious leaders in the dedication of Christ at all. God chose the ones
who were to take part in this momentous occasion not based on
position or outward appearances, but based on their hearts. Anna was
a very old woman who had dedicated her life to worshipping, fasting,
and praying. Simeon was described as being righteous and devout.
These were the ones whose hearts were open to what God was doing
in our world. They had eyes that were willing to see, ears that were
willing to hear, and mouths that were willing to boldly proclaim that
which the Spirit was leading them to share. God was able to use them

because they did not think highly of themselves, but highly of Him! They spent time with God and got to know Him. They emptied themselves out to God so that He could fill them back up with the Holy Spirit. Often, when we read about people like Simeon and Anna in the Bible, we feel like a relationship with God similar to theirs is unattainable. We are right if we, like the religious leaders of that day, become so distracted with what we want to do for God that we fail to see what He wants to do through us. God already has the plan! All we have to do is get close enough to Him that we can see how that plan is already at work and join in. Fall more in love with Jesus. Give more of yourself to God. Ask Him today to show you how.

Prayer and Praise:

_____

_____

_____

_____

_____

_____

_____

_____

_____

_____

_____

_____

_____

_____

_____

_____

_____

_____

King of the Jews

DECEMBER 19
6 DAYS UNTIL CHRISTMAS

After Jesus was born in Bethlehem in Judea, during the time of King Herod, Magi from the east came to Jerusalem and asked, "Where is the one who has been born King of the Jews? We saw his star in the east and have come to worship Him."
Matthew 2:1-2

Matthew is the only writer who mentions the account of the magi visitation. There is much scholarly debate about who the magi were, how many there were, where they specifically came from, how they learned about Christ, and when they came. Although there are some very logical hypotheses, the only truth we can believe with complete certainty is what we read in the Bible. Other historical documents are helpful in putting pieces of the puzzle together in regard to political and cultural events of that day, but we cannot completely rely on the accuracy of such documents as we can the Word of God. The word magi is plural so we know that there was more than one magus, but the Bible does not specifically tell us how many magi came. Later in the Scripture, we read that they gave Jesus gold, frankincense, and myrrh, leading some to guess that there were three magi, each giving their own gift. The idea that these visitors might be kings probably came about because magi were often chosen as counselors to kings because of their wisdom. Again, if we don't read it in the Bible, we can only make educated guesses. Historical, not biblical, definitions of the word magi tell us that their area of expertise was in the study of the stars. We know from Matthew's account that the magi came because of a star in the east. They already knew when they arrived in Jerusalem that the star meant that the King of the Jews had been born, but we can only guess how they learned this truth. We also know that it was their intent to worship Jesus, but we do not know anything else about their religious beliefs. We will talk in the days to come about Herod's response to the magi, and the age and location of Christ when the magi found Him. In regards to the magi, we may not have a complete picture, but it is as complete as it needs to be, according to God's wisdom. He didn't accidentally leave out some facts! Remember, with God nothing happens by chance. It will be fun someday in Heaven, though, to sit at our Heavenly Father's feet and listen as He fills in all the details for us!

Prayer and Praise:

_____

_____

_____

_____

_____

_____

_____

_____

_____

_____

_____

_____

_____

_____

_____

_____

Shepherd of My People

DECEMBER 20
5 DAYS UNTIL CHRISTMAS

When King Herod heard this he was disturbed, and all Jerusalem with him. When he had called together all the people's chief priests and teachers of the law, he asked them where the Christ was to be born. "In Bethlehem in Judea, they replied, "for this is what the prophet has written: But you, Bethlehem, in the land of Judah, are by no means least among the rulers of Judah; for out of you will come a ruler who will be the shepherd of my people Israel." Then Herod called the Magi secretly and found out from them the exact time the star had appeared.
Matthew 2:3-7

It disturbed King Herod that a baby had been born who was to shepherd the people of Israel because any such baby threatened his position as King. It disturbed the people of Jerusalem because they did not want anything to cause further strife in the already turbulent and complex political system. The chief priests and teachers of the law immediately knew where the Christ was to be born, but did not show any sign that they were joyful over the news of His birth. This is how the Savior found our world when He arrived. Many of the people who had the greatest reason to celebrate Jesus were either unhappy or indifferent about His birth. As a Christian who loves Christ with all of my heart, I am so thankful for the way that the shepherds, Simeon, Anna, and the magi worshipped Jesus when He was born! The world is not so different now than it was then. Many of the people who have the greatest cause to celebrate Jesus' birth ignore Him this time of year. Santa, gifts, parties, family and friends seem to distract and take priority. We all have a choice, though. We can choose to focus on Him more, to worship and adore Him more, to love Him more! Just by spending the time to read today's verses, you have made a choice that honors Christ. Honor Him in all of your choices this holiday season. Let us show Him that He is welcome, not only in our world, but in our hearts!

Prayer and Praise:

_____

_____

_____

_____

_____

_____

_____

_____

_____

_____

_____

_____

_____

_____

_____

_____

_____

_____

_____

_____

_____

_____

_____

King of Kings

DECEMBER 21
4 DAYS UNTIL CHRISTMAS

He sent them to Bethlehem and said, "Go and make a careful search
for the child. As soon as you find him, report to me, so that I too
may go and worship him." After they had heard the king, they went
on their way, and the star they had seen in the east went ahead of
them until it stopped over the place where the child was. When they
saw the star, they were overjoyed. On coming to the house, they saw
the child with his mother Mary, and they bowed down and
worshipped him. Then they opened their treasures and presented him
with gifts of gold and of incense and of myrrh. And having been
warned in a dream not to go back to Herod, they returned to their
country by another route.
Matthew 2:8-12

The magi went on their way, and, when they saw the star, they
were overjoyed. They weren't face to face with Jesus yet, but still,
they were **overjoyed!** What were they thinking as they followed the
star? Could they have known that they were about to meet God's
Son? Did they sense that they were approaching holy ground? I
wonder if they planned to fall on their knees before Him, or if His
majesty overtook them and worship flowed out of them
uncontrollably. We know that they did plan ahead of time to present
Jesus with the most precious gifts they possessed, gold, frankincense,
and myrrh. We have never seen Jesus face to face with our own eyes,
but if we know Him as Savior and Lord, someday we will! Are we

overjoyed at the prospect? Are we on a journey, traveling toward Him, anticipating what it will be like when we see Him for the first time? Have you thought about what you will do? Will you fall before Him like the magi, or will you run into His arms like a child who has been away from his or her father far too long? Will you weep with gratitude or will you laugh with joy? What treasure will you have for Him? The magi planned ahead, and so must we. Gold, frankincense, and myrrh are not an option. We will not be taking our worldly possessions with us because they have no eternal value. The only gifts that we will have to lay at Jesus' feet are the sincere acts of service and love we gave in His name while we were here on Earth, and the people we introduced to Him along the way. What treasures have you stored up in Heaven for the day that you will be face to face with Jesus? Spend your life on Jesus now so that in Heaven you will not be lacking in treasures to present to your King!

Prayer and Praise:

_____

_____

_____

_____

_____

_____

_____

_____

_____

_____

_____

_____

_____

Called Out of Egypt

DECEMBER 22
3 DAYS UNTIL CHRISTMAS

When they had gone, an angel of the Lord appeared to Joseph in a
dream. "Get up," he said, "take the child and his mother and escape
to Egypt. Stay there until I tell you, for Herod is going to search for
the child to kill him. " So he got up, took the child and his mother
during the night and left for Egypt, where he stayed until the death of
Herod. And so was fulfilled what the Lord had said through the
prophet: "Out of Egypt I called my son."
Matthew 2:13-15

The magi had already heard from God in a dream that they should
not go back to Herod, so they obediently returned to their country by
another route. Next, Joseph heard from God that Herod wanted to
kill Jesus and that he was to take the child and Mary and escape to
Egypt. I love how Joseph obeyed. He did not wait until morning so
that Jesus and Mary could get a good night's rest. He woke them up
right then! In the middle of the night, they left for Egypt. He did not
just obey, he obeyed quickly and completely. That is the kind of
obedience that God needs from us! What might have happened if
Joseph had hesitated or delayed? God would have found another way
to protect His Son, but then Joseph would have missed out on being
used by God in His plan. God deserves our total obedience, and we
don't want to miss out on the blessings that inevitably follow Godly
obedience. God still speaks! He instructs us through His Spirit, His
Word, prayer, and the Godly counsel of other believers. He will

never force obedience, but He will always bless it! What has God asked you to do that you are just not doing? Get up quickly, do it now, and wait to see how God will bless!

Prayer and Praise:

_____

_____

_____

_____

_____

_____

_____

_____

_____

_____

_____

_____

_____

_____

_____

_____

_____

_____

_____

_____

_____

_____

Our Only Comfort

DECEMBER 23
2 DAYS UNTIL CHRISTMAS

When Herod realized that he had been outwitted by the Magi, he was
furious, and he gave orders to kill all the boys in Bethlehem and its
vicinity who were two years old and under, in accordance with the
time he had learned from the Magi. Then what was said through the
prophet Jeremiah was fulfilled. "A voice is heard in Ramah, weeping
and great mourning, Rachel weeping for her children and refusing to
be comforted, because they are no more."
Matthew 2:16-18

The Magi visited Jesus in a house at some point after Mary's days
of purification were complete, and Jesus had been dedicated to the
Lord in the temple. We know that they visited after the dedication
because the Bible tells us that, after the Magi visited, God warned
Joseph to leave for Egypt, which he did immediately. There wouldn't
have been time for the dedication to occur after the Magi visited. We
know from Jewish custom that the purification was at least forty-one
days after Christ's birth. We see in today's text that the information
Herod received from the Magi led him to believe that Jesus was no
older than two years by the time that he realized he had been
outwitted. These facts reveal that the Magi did not visit Christ on the
night of His birth as our culture often depicts, but somewhere
between forty-one days and two years. Just because Herod had all
baby boys who were less than two killed doesn't mean that Jesus was
two. It just means that he was no older than two. In the referenced

prophecy, which is found in Jeremiah 31:15, Rachel, who had died giving birth to Benjamin in Ramah, is symbolic of Israel. Jacob buried her there and set up a memorial to her near Bethlehem where the slaughter took place. This is included in Matthew because it is a confirmation of prophecy that would be well understood by the Jews, for whom Matthew was written. For us, it is a reminder that weeping and mourning in our world are constants that will not be comforted until Jesus wipes away all of our tears in Heaven. The hope that we have to offer those who are hurting around us is that Jesus has promised never to leave us alone in our sorrows. He walks with us through each trial. Shine the light of Christ to a world desperately in need of the comfort that only He can bring.

Prayer and Praise:

_____

_____

_____

_____

_____

_____

_____

_____

_____

_____

_____

_____

_____

_____

_____

_____

_____

Jesus of Nazareth

DECEMBER 24
1 DAY UNTIL CHRISTMAS

After Herod died, an angel of the Lord appeared in a dream to Joseph in Egypt and said, "Get up, take the child and his mother and go to the land of Israel. But when he heard that Archelaus was reigning in Judea in place of his father Herod, he was afraid to go there. Having been warned in a dream, he withdrew to the district of Galilee, and he went and lived in a town called Nazareth. So was fulfilled what was said through the prophets: "He will be called a Nazarene."
Matthew 2:19-23

Jesus, Mary, and Joseph were in Egypt waiting on God to tell them the next step of His plan. God did not tell them ahead of time how long they were to stay, but He had been faithful to lead them from the very beginning of their lives together in Nazareth. They understood that not knowing what the future held was okay because the One who holds the future in His hands was in charge. In God's perfect timing, He called His Son out of Egypt and led Him right back to Nazareth just as scripture had prophetically foretold. Each move along the way was mapped out by God and followed obediently by Joseph. God works the same way with us. It would be much too overwhelming if He revealed His entire plan for us all at once. In His infinite wisdom, He gives us one step of the plan at a time. It is so important that we stay close enough to God that we can hear His voice as He leads, and then obediently follow Him without question. It is difficult to hear someone speaking to us who we never spend time with. God is unchanging. When we are not close to Him, it is not because He has moved away from us. It is because we have moved away from Him. It is up to us to spend time with God each day in prayer and in His Word. We should be so familiar with His voice that even His whispers are loud and clear to us. A relationship like that takes time to develop. Start where you are today and do just a little more to get closer to God. Ask Him for His help with this, knowing that it is His great desire to draw you to Himself!

Prayer and Praise:

_____

_____

_____

_____

_____

_____

_____

_____

_____

_____

_____

_____

_____

_____

_____

_____

_____

_____

The Grace of God

DECEMBER 25
CHRISTMAS DAY

When Joseph and Mary had done everything required by the Law of
the Lord, they returned to Galilee to their own town of Nazareth.
And the child grew and became strong; he was filled with wisdom,
and the grace of God was upon Him.
Luke 2:39-40

Happy Birthday Jesus! Christmas day has finally arrived- the
special day we set aside each year to remember Jesus' birthday. Our
family has prayed for you each day this month that God's Word
would come alive in your heart and that you would fall more in love
with Jesus than you have ever been before. This month, we have read
about Mary and Joseph and their incredible journey with God as they
witnessed the birth of Jesus. Now, it is time for them to return to
Galilee to their own town of Nazareth. The story is far from over,
though. Jesus grew and became strong; He was filled with wisdom,
and the grace of God was upon Him. He lived a perfect, sinless life
and willingly gave Himself for you and for me on the cross so that we
can have a relationship with God. He lives in Heaven...for now. He
has promised to come back for us and has asked us to be ready!
Tomorrow is a new day. As you pack up your Christmas decorations
and start thinking about the New Year, include Christ in your
thoughts and plans. He is just as worthy of our praise and worship
everyday as He is today! Maybe you aren't in the habit of spending
time reading the Bible and praying every day. Continue to read Luke,

and find out exactly what Jesus did while He was here on earth and what He is doing now in Heaven. He is working His plan out on Earth and wants you to be a part of it! He created you to join Him in His Kingdom's work, and you won't be truly happy any other way. To God be the glory for your life and all that He will accomplish through you if you are completely surrendered to Him!

Prayer and Praise:

_____

_____

_____

_____

_____

_____

_____

_____

_____

_____

_____

_____

_____

_____

_____

_____

_____

_____

_____

_____

_____

_____

_____

_____

_____

ABOUT THE AUTHOR

Ronda is the wife of Chuck Davenport and the mother of five children- Chad, Anna, Zachary, Joshua, and Jacob. She lives in Georgia, where she and her husband were born and raised. She earned her degree in elementary education at the University of Georgia and taught elementary school until she had children of her own. She now devotes her time to her family and the Prayer Ministry at First Baptist Church Woodstock. Ronda is passionate about her relationship with Jesus Christ, prayer, and sharing the God's love with the world.

Made in the USA
Middletown, DE
28 November 2022

16259299R00033